the Underground

Philosophy of

Education

by J. Speeks

KOBALT BOOKS

Kobalt Books LLC
Philadelphia | St. Louis

THE UNDERGROUND PHILOSOPHY OF EDUCATION
Copyright © 2011 by J. Speeks
ISBN-13: 978-0-9820330-7-4 / ISBN-10: 0-9820330-7-9

Cover Design by Thomas Roach
Book Edited by Cedric Mixon
Library of Congress Control Number: 2011925204

For information:
Kobalt Books
P.O. Box 1062
Bala Cynwyd, PA 19004
Printed in the U.S.A
www.**kobaltbooks**.com

Published by Kobalt Books L.L.C.
An original publication of Kobalt Books L.L.C.

Table of Contents

Chapter 1: The Philosophy – Wait, Take, Share -------- page 7

Chapter 2: Teachers – Weed Them Out ---------------- page 29

Chapter 3: Students – Signs of Ignorance -------------- page 43

Chapter 4: Parents – Unknowledgeable
Persistence ----------------------- page 55

Chapter 5: The Administration –
Blame or Responsibility ----------------- page 75

Chapter 6: Welcome to Oz ------------------------------- page 85

Chapter 7: If Education Was a Pill ---------------------- page 99

PREFACE

The Underground Philosophy of Education is a testament to honest answers about the concerns of the future of the American Education system from the front line. Given in the viewpoint of a certified teacher, it expresses the joys, sorrows, and anxieties of ensuring a future for all of today's youth and tomorrow's leaders. It strips the education profession free of politics and bureaucracy and presents an open and honest look through the eyes of a dedicated educator. It is more of a personal journal of opinions based on the experiences of one man, and is not meant to be the voice of every educator. The author is an African American male teacher who has risen from the streets of public housing to a successful career. His successes are modest in monetary value, but monumental in the height that he has risen over the stereotypes and statistics of black males; and he hopes to be the example for other males or any student who is categorized as being "at risk" of not succeeding. Witness the philosophy of education from a black perspective and see that it is really a human perspective. It erases lines and boundaries and presents uncensored opinions based on researched and proven ideals on school improvement. This book will turn the Education System on its ear as the realities are revealed with no threat of liability, which so often silences many advocates for education. As questions and curiosities increase about the underpinnings of the educational process, this book becomes an important source of insight that can initiate positive talks about real solutions. The best part is that the book comes out without previous censorship through any educational institutions that might hinder the rough and raw content that exists as **the Underground Philosophy of Education**.

For My Family

Chapter 1: The Philosophy – Wait, Take, Share

Now, the real deal of education can be discussed in simpler terms than pedagogical creeds and differentiated instruction of the sort. I would like to let the reader know how I decomposed the professional talk to what I will call the casual language to which one can relate and [simply] understand better. Just in case there is any mystery, I am a child of public housing and of a single parent family of eight children; so while I was growing up, I was clueless to any words similar to epistemology. In the field, I often had to break down the million dollar words for myself in order to connect what I see with what I know. And so, the following thoughts were constructed in the meantime to create my creed for education.

The development of a child is one of the major areas of focus to address in presenting a philosophical stance on education. To that, I believe that a child development is due in part to interactions with the environment. Scientists have conducted extensive research concerning the "nature verses nurture" theory, which analyzes whether a child naturally acts the way he or she does, or if their environment influences them.

Tell me, how many people operate totally from natural instinct, with no evidence of change or development through experience? Or, how many people go solely by what they pick up from their environment and never show any evidence of instinctive or natural behavior? The battle to base education on either nature or nurture is senseless because it is clearly a mixture. I also talked about how a child develops through social interactions. One can see that a child's educational experience seems to be based solely on interaction. Can you think of a child who comes to school specifically to read, do math, spell, and memorize countries everyday; a child who never thinks about when he or she is going to see a friend, girlfriend, or have to face an enemy?

In my experiences, a child mainly comes to school to talk with friends. Some keep their grades up in order to maintain freedoms and rewards, but if grades had no bearings on a child (i.e. passing, failing, or sports eligibility) how do you think report cards would look? To the child, school is not fundamentally about education and we need to keep that in mind. Students already know why they're coming and stressing the importance only effects a few.

Continuing on similar lines as to why students come to school, one might also think about why students behave the way they do when they are there? If they have their own reasons to come, it is almost certain that those reasons will control how they act. In my creed, I stated that behavior is intrinsic. I think that what a child does comes from them and only them. If you study the behavior of a child (good or bad), you can see that they know exactly what they're doing and the consequences of their actions. Even in law, the few times a person was not held accountable for their actions were if their insanity plea was actually proven. Otherwise, people in life and children in school are aware of what they are doing. The important question is to figure out why they choose to do the wrong thing instead of the right thing. That is a million dollar question that I'm not sure has one blanket answer. When I think about what made me choose to do the right thing when I was surrounded by so much wrong doing, I don't think I would answer it the same as any other person who went through similar instances. Besides, there were times I chose to do the wrong thing and it was solely by the grace of God that I am here today in this position. I could have easily been in the position that would have forced outsiders to ask the question, "How can a person let himself fall so far down the destructive path of life?" However, I did discover an idea that I felt covered a lot of the feelings I had in life, right and wrong. The information captured me so greatly that it was imperative that I add it into the creed.

During my undergraduate years I came across a psychosocial theory by a philosopher named Eric Erikson that intrigued me. He talked about the crises that children faced in development. When you think about students, especially in middle school, who does not get the word CRISIS ringing in their minds? To break it all down into a personal perspective, in school I will admit that I had issues in regards to trust, believing in my ability, knowing what type of person I wanted to be, being accepted, and most of all, not ending up like my father. Those were just a few of the crises of which I felt that I faced. It has all the workings of such categories that

Erikson discussed in his theory: trust, autonomy, initiative, industry, identity, intimacy, generativity, and integrity. And as I think of them all, I realize there is one single aspect that can change them all—ethnicity. That caused an explosion of emotion when that went through my mind. It's an amazing thing to keep in mind being a teacher. It affects so much as far as the approach to the individual student that may have many crises going on in very different ways. Finding the psychosocial theory was very important to me because it gave meaning to some things about which I felt confused when I was young.

After discussing the development of a child, my creed went into the role of schools. Again, the creed is a personal declaration so it is relative to my experiences from the time that I was in school to now while I am a teacher. One quality that I described that a school should be, is transformational. The term involves how there is a direct connection between the student and the teacher, curriculum, or any other important aspect of education. The child cannot be told that they need an education simply to get ahead. The child has to develop a belief in education. The child must think that they are responsible for the outcomes of their lives in accordance with the education they receive. And one may ask how old must a child be in order to develop such a complex idea? I say as old as a child must be to know that he or she is good at something. Once I was convinced that learning was not hard, it made things look totally different to me.

It also goes back to Erikson's category of autonomy verses doubt. The negative has been what I have seen as the biggest determinant between whether a child liked school or not. The fear of being embarrassed if he or she cannot find the answer goes as far as causing a child to deliberately get him or herself in trouble to avoid the situation. Thankfully enough I chose to feign sickness instead of acting out with a negative behavior. However, once things didn't seem so difficult to learn, I actually wanted to go to school. Imagine that; a child WANTING to go to school to learn. If only there was a drug that we could prescribe to stir up the desire to learn we wouldn't need Ritalin. However, since there is no pharmaceutical remedy, I must recall what really worked for me.

The term dialectical describes what I thought was a good way to capture my interests. It involves the use of strategies. I know the use of the word strategies may be met with much kudos from educators, but hold on to those for now. I hesitate because I am sure my view of strategies is a little different from the accepted view of strategies. I'm not even going to call them strategies. I will refer to them as engagements. Children like to play games and strategies are supposed to be fun and interesting ways to teach. Now, think about games you have played in your life and strategies you have used or seen in the classroom. Are the two related? Let's be real. Some of the strategies that have been created are neither fun nor interesting. Yes, they are a hit at the professional development groups, but whom are they supposed to be targeting? Let me give an example of the difference.

Strategy—think, pair, share—pretty interesting but not the most fun activity. It's where you think about the question and write a response, pair up with another student and combine answers, and share the results with the rest of the class.

I have seen where the kids more often "wait, take, share." They will wait for other groups to get an answer, take the answer, and (if called on first) share a stolen answer. The reason is that such strategy is seen by the students as a way to try to trick them into learning, so they try to trick the teacher into thinking that they are actually participating.

Game—heads up, seven up—wonderful game that all students love to play and forces social interaction. The only problem is that it has no academic merit. However, I adapted the game just a little. Five problems are given and five students are chosen (seven may be too much in this method). As the game goes, the five chosen students then touch the thumb of a person whose head is on his or her desk. The people chosen have to figure out who picked them. If they are correct, they go up. If they are incorrect, the person who chose them stays up. With my game, I kept the same rules, except that there were two chances to be correct. If you are incorrect about who chose you, you can solve one of the problems to stay up there. If you are correct, the person who chose you can solve a problem to stay there. It is a great review "strategy" but the kids know it as a game that they are used to and have no problem playing it or trying to trick the teacher into thinking that they are playing. It also forces them to pay attention if they want the chance to stay in the game. Don't get me wrong; I think strategies are a great way to engage students in learning. However, we shouldn't use things that sound good to other teachers or administrators. We should use things that are proven to get the students hooked. The word "strategy" would not even register in a child's mind as quickly as the word "game." The child is whom we should keep in mind first and foremost.

Following the lines of keeping the child in mind, I would like to address another term that I used in creed to describe the role of the school. I stated that it should be dialogical, meaning that the teacher is seen as human and learns as the student learns. The mentioned term is very delicate, however. One has to keep in mind the purpose and extent. It is not intended to make friends or be unprofessional. Showing human qualities are only to shed the pre-conceived notions that all students in the world have about teachers. I am a teacher now, but I had the same ideas when I was in school. Do the teachers ever go home? Do teachers wear anything besides "teacher clothes"? Such questions show how disconnected students are to the reality that teachers are human too. It does not help how the community and society places them on a tight rope like the media does to superstars. Too bad the pay scale between the two was tipped. Getting back to the matter at hand, however, there is a huge disconnection between students and teachers simply because the students don't see teachers as normal human beings. It is said how it is hard to understand someone if you cannot relate to them. Often, students come in with the mindset that they are not going to be capable of relating to the teacher, which puts everyone at a disadvantage from the beginning. But, after the student learns that the teacher is normal as well, it changes the whole dynamic of the classroom environment. On seldom occasions, I would drift from the lesson if someone mentioned an unrelated topic. Then I would simply let them know we need to get back on task, but I just wanted to talk about the other subject and I could not wait. Children can never wait until the appropriate time to talk to a friend about certain things. By me showing that I am the same way, it presents a human side; a relatable side. It does not have to be a big deal. In fact, it is better if it not be made a big deal to be human, because that can lead to problems with classroom management as well. However, each time you make a small deal, they wait attentively for the next time; some actually staying attentive enough to learn a thing or two. I have seen that some educators try too hard to be one way or the other. Such behavior builds the "not human" or even "holier than thou" attitude that students have generalized being possessed by all teachers.

To finish off the discussion of the role of the school, I visit the qualities of a school being reconstructive and emancipating. Once the student has established a connection to the school and thus decided to learn on his or her own accord, they will see things in a new light. It will begin rebuilding their thoughts in every aspect of their lives. They will be release from a defeated mindset and be determined to embrace excellence. Consider my story. I started out as the fifth child of eight children in the projects. My surroundings showed me that people in my neighborhood are supposed to fight, steal, or sell drugs to make it. At school, even though I shed the mentality of the poor and worked to excel, my classmates reminded me that I was far different. The black students wondered how I could be so smart, coming from the projects. I definitely didn't belong in that group. The white students wondered why I was in the gifted classes when I was so poor.

However, I saw things in the light of one day being in the place where both groups would look up to me as intently as they looked down on me. I had gone as far as thinking of ways to use my knowledge to manipulate. It is a sad confession, but I felt that my knowledge was true power that I could use to my advantage. Can one make a judgment on such a mindset? In one light, it has a ring to it of a comic book villain. However, it made me an honors' graduate in high school and college and I never have provoked the wrath of a single caped crusader. All I know is that I chose to get an education and that put power in my hands to become successful.

My successes in life led to me wanting to help others reach their goals. I chose to be an educator because I felt that I could help a child get past the crossroad of excelling or failing; constructive thought or destructive behavior; life or death. A description that I found that matched my ideals is the passionate participant and facilitator. I am not here to control the students like a dictator, but direct their thinking and actions; being sensitive to the crises that they may encounter and being directly involved in their lives and well-being.

There is a lot that educational research can do to help with some of the problems that we face in the classrooms, but it is important to realize that every single student is different. One of the only common threads that bind them is the fact that they all have a story that tells who they are. We don't write it for them, so we should not try to. We need to encourage them to write their own stories and make them fairy tales so that they can live happily ever after. For this, I added the implications of the creed and what it means for the classroom. I stated that differentiated instruction is vital to ensure that everyone is being accommodated. Differentiation oftentimes means lessons for different learning abilities, whether it is learning styles or even the rate of mastery. It mainly deals with cognitive capabilities. However, my take on differentiated instruction covers a lot more ground. To me its adding relevance to a child's life by including things to which they are familiar. Linking graphs and charts to the sports that the children enjoy; finding grammar or literary devices in popular songs. I went as far as to linking how the science of sound waves allowed me to hear students whispering even though my back was turned on them. I also went as far as saying that just talking to kids sometimes, in more of a causal manner, would even help. It goes back to the persona that children have about their teachers and how it needs to be broken. It shows that the teacher is trying to meet them on a more level field no matter their ability. Again, it is the little things that make the monumental difference. The elaborate plans, curriculum maps to follow along, visual aids, and other complex designs are great to fill the room up and impress the visiting administration. But, ask the children what they are going to do with all of the wonderful instructional aides once they go back to their neighborhoods.

So as I reach my conclusion, I show you that this underground philosophy of education that I have does not come from a desire to point out anyone like a disgruntled postal worker or something, but to share with readers a true creed that I have with more practical implications. The ideas were initially researched and supported, but it would be a tragedy not for me to explain in-depth. Though the research gives relevance to this book, I reiterate that the purpose is for discussion. The next section moves away the basic principles of the creed and focuses more on experiences in education and more generalized implications. Nothing is to be taken as researched facts, but pay close attention, because there is truth in observation. Keep in mind that the experiences are based on a middle school level, which may or may not present drastic differences.

Chapter 2: Teachers – Weed Them Out

The underground philosophy was created to cover things that are not formally researched and addressed in an academic setting without some sort of backlash. What a teacher goes through is critical in my philosophy because if everyone were a little more sensitive to the teacher, it would send a positive ripple through the current state of education as a whole. Any new teachers or potential teachers should pay close attention to this section, because it is something that they don't teach you in any course. However, results may vary; so read responsively.

Think about how often it has been said that a teacher does not get paid clearly enough for what they do. How many would agree or disagree? The question is met with much criticism. Some say that a teacher's job is not hard and they only have to know basic subject knowledge. Some say that teachers should be grateful to get all the holidays that a student gets. It is a common belief that a teacher's job is mildly difficult and to complain means that they are only in it for the money anyway. But, really think about it. The pay schedule has never had a drastic rise, so teachers know what they are getting into beforehand. For nearly all teachers, it is never about the money. However, what would happen if the payroll method was changed? What if a teacher could clock in and out for every moment he or she is doing something work related? What if a teacher was paid every time a paper is graded, a parent is called, new lesson plans are written after school, an activity is chaperoned, open house is held, or anything else that concerns the school. At a descent hourly rate, a teacher may come out as well as the more competitive careers such as doctors, lawyers, etc. Yet, teachers spend hours after school, on the weekend, and even during the holidays preparing and even checking up on students because that is what teaching is about. It seems to be greatly taken for granted.

Teachers also go beyond the call on a regular basis to make sure the students can have the best educational experience as possible. They act as more than an educator during the course of the day. With all the crises that children come to school with, teachers also carry roles much like parents, friends, counselors, and other support for the students. Take a poll. Ask how many teachers have taken money from their own pockets (even as they are said to complain about salary) to buy things for a child who may not have as much as the rest of the students? How much of teachers' concern has resulted in home visits? How many teachers spend their weekends and afternoons watching their students play sports and other extracurricular activities? Clearly those things are not written in the contract as a requirement, but to the truly concerned teachers, it matters. To the teacher, every student is an offspring. How often is the case where one is trying to take care of seventy to a hundred offspring? Teachers approach their jobs as if they are doing just that. Every parent that is reading, imagine that you had almost one hundred children for which to care. Such is a monumental task. More so, the task increases every year because the previous kids are not forgotten and continues be a concern as much as the new kids who are just now coming to the classroom. My philosophy is that teaching is one profession that is more than just a paycheck; it is a life calling. However, it is met with many adversities.

As a teacher, it is disheartening to anticipate going into the line of fire each day, but the truth of the matter is that sometimes, it cannot be described any other way. As discussed earlier, teachers come in with the biggest open hearts, taking in students as children and worrying for them just as much as parents and other family members. However, at the same time teachers have great anxiety about the outcome of each day with faculty meetings, parent conferences, and even impromptu meetings with administrators. An experience that can exemplify the circumstances is the beginning of the year faculty meeting, where it is required to view a video on ethics. It is a requirement to see all the things you cannot do as if one has to be reminded how to act professionally. However, the video itself is not the most insulting part of the experience. As the video winds on showing the teachers how to have manners, when do the students, parents, and other community members watch their video on how to have manners? When are they given a list of what not to do or say that is unethical to the teachers? There are no set parameters for the amount of conflict and criticism that an outside figure can bring into the schools, but teachers are strictly monitored even to the extent to which they can tell the truth.

There have been many instances when an irate parent has stirred up controversy in the schools, making it school officials job to play damage control to calm the parent down. The parent is also mildly held accountable for such a disruption. Yet, there have been instances where a teacher just gives an honest opinion to a parent, and loses his or her job. It seems as though the more commotion a parent causes, the more the system works to satisfy them; but the more commotion a teacher causes (no matter how innocent), the more the teacher is seen as a threat to the learning community and must be quickly silenced.

Let's use rapper, Eminem, as an example. Being an educator, it is tough to hold such a high respect for a person who has the lyrical content that is very lewd, but one must respect his drive. Fortunately for Eminem, he has the power to strike back when criticized and further increase his popularity. Most of his celebrity is based on his being able to withstand the opposition. One particular instance was when his lyrics was said to heavily and wrongly influence children. Emimen quickly turned the issue back to the question of where is the parenting? It is a close relationship to how things occur in the education field. Any problem goes wrong inside or outside the classroom, the blame most often falls on the teacher most closely tied to the circumstance. However, it is definitely not possible to fight back or gain popularity from standing against the problem— unless a book is written that supports the truth!

Certainly when it comes down to it, teaching is still a job. Teachers are treated like workers with very high expectations. However, teachers do not have the usual supervisors and managers. Teachers face scrutiny from parents, administrators, board members, legislators all the way up to the federal level, communities, students, and even each other at times. How well is that scale balanced between responsibility and reward? It does not seem to equal out much.

The teaching profession has been described as simply educating the students. Give the students the knowledge and let them continue on in life. But, the facets of the job are much more complex than it sounds. The knowledge is given through a curriculum prescribed by the "experts". The fashion in which to deliver the knowledge is also prescribed by the "experts". The stated prescriptions are then sold to the administration; who, in turn, feeds it to the teachers. The progress is monitored by a series of test (also made by the "experts"). The results tell whether or not a teacher is doing his or her job and if he or she should keep the job. The parent monitors progress to see if the child is acquiring the knowledge and to see what the teacher's problem is if the child is not. The parents group up as a community to collectively demand that the teacher's problem is solved. The legislation listens to the community. The teachers expose each other out of fear of the community and legislation. The scenario is a seemingly drastic generalization, but someone has to cut through the fat and fluff and get to the heart of the situation. The question becomes where the teacher fits in the whole equation besides the scapegoat for society's ills. It does not mean that all teachers are blamed for what's wrong, but it does seem like the little matters (that doesn't even have to be a problem) are over exaggerated to take the attention from elsewhere. Sadly, the teacher continues to take on the same obstacles continuously because they do not want to fail the children that they teach. Obviously, the focus of teachers is different from everyone else. Sure, everyone had the same general goal to make sure that all students excel in school and ultimately in life; but the means to that goal is a constant scramble.

Please do not get the idea that all teachers should be seen as "sent straight from the heavens and can do no wrong." Teachers have setbacks. It has been said and I cannot totally deny that some teachers are in the profession for vacation time and easy money. Some think that it is easy to become a teacher. Such has caused an increased call for certification. What more can be asked of a teacher to prove his or her worth? So much attention is being paid to ensure that a teacher is the expert and will do the best job asked, the real evidence is missed. When you have teachers who spend hours beyond the regular work day preparing for the next day, uses money from his or her pockets for supplies for the class or personal supplies for less fortunate students, fights for students who have been labeled as a "lost cause" by some, you have your evidence. Unconcerned teachers can be weeded out easily through innovation. Ask them what are they willing to do to better relate to the students; not just trying to please the administration; but, actually having a lasting impression on an "at-risk" student who wants to change their life in order to maintain approval by the teacher. True teaching changes lives and true innovation sets up the opportunity. If you want accountability, ask the students what influences them to succeed. Anytime a student achieves and contributes, a part of the achievement to a favorite teacher shows that the teacher has done the job for which all teachers should strive. Yet, I only state an opinion.

Who has the right idea of how to get where we need to be in education? The answer to the previous question needs careful consideration. The teacher is very important, but how much do they matter in the total scheme of things? This particular chapter was not to say that the teacher is the only important part of the education process. But certainly teachers should not be seen as THE problem every time life is not perfect in the world of education. Every person involved is important. The key to success is that there must remain a high respect for all roles—even the student.

Chapter 3: Students – Signs of Ignorance

Let me start off by saying that in no way is this resentment towards children. I value being a teacher, and the students give me reward enough to want to continue. This chapter is simply to offer insight on how students operate in the experiences that I have had. Keep in mind that students come from many different backgrounds. They also, as mentioned previously, have their own personal crises that they face as they enter the classroom. Through it all, they oftentimes seem to be forced to learn on a daily basis. We all know that anytime we feel as if we are forced to do something, it automatically makes us hate it. Then to top it all, the teachers are the first faces that they see daily on their hated paths. So naturally, some of the hatred tends to spread towards the teacher. Not to say that it manifests in any physical acts, but it can cause a schism in the student-teacher relationship. From there, the interactions become very interesting.

We cannot truly hold the student accountable for every single belief that they hold, because it most assuredly has come from the home. However, we can hold them responsible for their actions. It brings back the nature verses nurture idea. They may have been nurtured into some of their beliefs, but it becomes a natural instinct to know when an action that is blatantly wrong has been committed. Yet, students have very peculiar behavior that begs the question of what are they thinking? I speak not of the things that are possible, only of the things I have seen; students confronting teachers, threatening teachers, physically striking teachers, lying on teachers; the list goes on. One can only wonder why they think this behavior is okay. A number of those students do not see that they committed any transgression. And as the teacher, what can truly be done? Classroom management is supposed to take care of the matter, but classroom management is a temporary fix until another incident happens. It does not change the belief system of the child; meaning that if the child continues to miss the error of his or her ways, he or she will never think that the action is wrong. Also, if the teacher specifically addresses that the issue is deeper, they enter a realm of legal boundaries that could even lead to the loss of a job. Where is the line drawn to where someone steps in on behalf of the teacher? Not to say that a teacher has no support or backing whatsoever. We all have to pick our battles carefully, but it seems that sometimes the battle is forced upon a teacher without a strategy for defense. One wonders, are students capable of understanding just how greatly their actions affect the livelihood of a teacher?

Not trying to sound like the clichéd teacher, I do think that all of the students I've come across were smart children. I do not base this from academic merit alone; I base it on my interactions with the student. The question was posed if students are capable of understanding the effects of their actions. I cannot think of one student who did not understand. I read a book once saying how a child chooses the behavior because there is always a purpose behind it. My underground philosophy agrees with such statement. I am a firm believer that a lot of the actions taken by students (no matter how poorly thought through) had a purpose. With learning being a synthesis of information gathered to reach a higher understanding, all of my students have shown a capability to learn. When a child takes the fact the he does not quite catch on to math, he may attempt to divert attention away from himself by provoking another student; that is intelligence. When a child has learned that his parents believe everything he says and lies on a teacher, knowing that his parents will believe him; that is intelligence. Doing something harmful like sticking a screwdriver into an electrical outlet is a sign of ignorance. Twisting a teacher's words just enough to where it almost makes what was said sound true, but can be used against a teacher to get out of trouble is a sign of intelligence. Don't get me wrong, I don't condone a child's manipulation against a teacher. I am teacher for goodness sakes! I am stating that if a child can put that much mental energy into getting out of learning, he still shows the capacity to learn. The energy must be channeled in a way that the student becomes aware of the capability and uses it for good. So before you are quick to label a child, think about the actions he or she has chosen on a daily basis and ask yourself if those actions show careful synthesis of information into a higher understanding? You may be surprised to think that what happened was the child actually outsmarted you! The idea may seem to be out in left field, but the point is just that no matter what action a child takes (good or bad), one must look at the complexity of the situation and see indeed the child shows a capacity for knowledge synthesis. What is left is to find a way to use the ability for good and not bad. In no way should it be used as an excuse for the child not to accept responsibility for his actions.

Is it possible to use what a child is familiar with to channel their abilities, even if they do not follow the most appropriate behavior? The question is very difficult to answer. Here is where your academic saviors such as differentiated instruction fall short. Some children are so self-involved that the run of the mill teacher strategies are equivalent to smoke and mirrors and have no relevance to them. A child's self-involvement usually includes the home life and/or social life. The behavior of a child is based mainly on the same two sources. The question is, are teacher strategies based on those same sources? It is unfair to judge teacher strategies as ineffective based on previous statements because it would be impossible to develop all instruction around every single child's home life or social life. Plus, do we really want to bring some of the children's home lives inside the classroom? I guess one cannot present such a complex issue without keying in on a point. The idea is to remain aware of the influences of child. One must learn as much about a child as they can in order to get a better understanding of what baggage with which a child is coming into the classroom. However, there is no way a teacher can tackle these issues alone. A teacher and a counselor together may even have a difficult time. My philosophy follows the old saying that it takes a village to raise a child. There has to be an overflow of support for the child. I am sure there are many people who can step in and show a child where he or she went wrong. What a child also needs is to know the he is normal no matter what circumstance he comes from, and that a successful education can change things. A child needs an outlet. I can say for certain that having an outlet really made a difference in my life. The outlet does not necessarily have to be an extracurricular activity or anything else that can put a strain on a child's resources. I feel an outlet is anything that opens the child up to considering going the right way in his or her actions. I offer a greater explanation through some problems that I have seen in the classroom.

There are always few students that are labeled as the "problem" students. I will agree as well that when those particular children came to my classroom, they indeed caused problems. However, I decided I would try some different methods to see if they caused problems to mask their inabilities, or merely to hide their abilities. On different occasions, I would level with the students on how I knew what they meant when they tried to say rude comments over my head. I would let them know that I was aware when they were trying to show off for a certain student. There were even occasions that if a child tried to get smart with me, I would show them that I could be smarter. None of the actions taken would be public. I just wanted the students to know that I understand what is going on and it is not necessary. Then I challenge them to try to get the same attention by doing the right thing. If they want to talk out, then talk out with an answer. If they could not stay in their seat, then they could constantly come to the board to work out an example. Simple alternatives as mentioned offers an outlet to help the student channel their ability the right way and still witness the outcome that their home life or social life has conditioned them to work towards. Keep in mind, to pull off these goals effectively, you must be extra sensitive to the students as not to cross any boundaries. You must also be careful not to give the student too much ground to cross boundaries as well. In all, the careful execution of real life "instructional strategies" will make the educational experience a more pleasant one

for both teacher and student.

Chapter 4: Parents – Unknowledgeable Persistence

I have found in my profession that one of the most delicate situations to handle as a teacher is dealing with a parent. Even though parent involvement is considered one of the most effective methods of behavior management, it is also one of the most apprehensive moves to make as a teacher; the reason being the uncertainty of the cooperativeness of the parents or the uncertainty of the primary motive the parents may have. Such uncertainty comes with the vast differences in each parent. Just like the student, the parents come to the school with very diverse backgrounds and very adult crises that they are dealing with on top of the issue of the child's educational status. If teachers find it important that parents are sensitive to their needs, they must also be sensitive. Parents have equally challenging responsibilities as anyone else. In fact, we all should approach each situation with a mindset that the person next to us has equally challenging responsibilities and may be masking equally difficult crises. The only disadvantage that a teacher has is that the parent is not bound to any strict codes of professionalism and conducts outside of the common laws that rule society—meaning that a parent can push the situation as far to the edge as they desire as long as it does not break any common law. Teachers face much more scrutiny in the way that they can handle a situation. Parents who are aware of the advantage are typically the ones that cause the most problems in the learning environment. However, parents that are ignorant to the fact can cause problems as well. In all, the main categories of parents can be broken according to the potential to cast a cloud over the education process. As the groups are discussed, a parent might want to see what type he or she may be. The category that seems the most untrue or insulting to a reader might actually be the particular group to which one belongs—just an opinion.

First of all, I would really like to praise the parents that work with the teachers and effectively solve any issues in the most diplomatic and professional manners. They are truly strong foundations that which a truly successful educational experience is built. However, I have seen some parents whose involvement is more detrimental than constructive. The parent shows true concern with the child's outcome, but has a cloudy viewpoint as to how to reach the desired goal. This parent's persistence overshadows the responsibility he or she has in maintaining success in the student and places all responsibility on the teacher; blaming the teacher for any and all points of weakness in the student. The persistent parent can follow two paths. One path is the unknowledgeable persistence where the parent continually calls for conferences to discuss an issue; only the parent is not very articulate and may not even have a point for persistence besides hoping that the involved educators make sure that the desired goal is reached by any means. Interaction with the unknowledgeable persistent parent is very wasteful due to the fact that the parent does not present a solution; just very extensive and unrelated arguments yielding no room for time to actually problem-solve. The result usually includes an idol threat of higher authority or the parent eventually realizing that the child is in the best hands and the battle ceases.

The opposite of the unknowledgeable persistent parent is the seemingly all- knowing persistent parent. For flattery, I called this parent the omniscient parent. The problem with the omniscient parent is that he or she knows much to do about nothing. This parent has studied the procedures, protocol, hierarchy, etc. Still, the most important thing that this parent knows is that his or her child is mostly the one in need of special attention (so to speak). Most often, the parent is the one of child with behavior issues, whose brushes with administration has lead to host of knowledge about the system. So instead of getting to the heart of the problem—the child, the parent has mastered a way to get around the problem and a lot of times, place the blame and responsibility back on the teacher or school. This type of parent fosters the belief that there are teachers who spend years of preparation, field experience, certification, and so on, just to pick on a particular child. The more frightening thing is that often the solution to a problem with the parent is in the parent's favor. I try to be objective about most things, but I would believe that such outcome inadvertently states that the parent was right; there have been a small number of cases where teachers spent the majority of their careers, harassing children. The grimmest realization of all is that the parent has been repeatedly sided with in such a matter. It is the aforementioned situation that put a dent in the positive flow of learning. Imagine the anticipation for the upcoming day, week, or year considering the previous. Still, such parents are only a fraction of the personality types that a teacher encounters.

Another set of parents that exists are the passive parents. Passive parents are those seldom seen. Not being able to reach a parent is detrimental because it causes a lack of knowledge of the background of a child when trying to construct the proper means of accommodation. It is a huge disconnect in the educational process. Yet it can be one of the easiest issues to tackle as far as educational improvement. I feel that improvement will reach a new level if we had one hundred percent participation from parents. However, passive parents are resistant to such outcome. The type of passive parent can be further broken down into two subgroups as well. I consider them as the unknowledgeable passive parent and the knowledgeable passive parent. There is not much to say about the unknowledgeable passive parents. They seem to sit and let the world pass them by. They do not seem to have any part in the educational process whatsoever. They often leave the teacher or administrator to do whatever is needed to solve the problem with no objection. There are many deeper issues behind this type of parent that would probably take another book to discuss. They simply are not involved, period.

Though they may not stir any discontent in the learning environment directly, their lack of involvement is a hindrance to the educators. However, their opposites pose a greater threat.

The darker side of the passive parent is the knowledgeable passive parent. They are not given the title "omniscient" simply because such title is used to describe the persistent. However, the knowledgeable passive parent has just as much of an insight to the procedures and protocol as the omniscient parent. The difference is that the passive parent constantly eludes the interaction with school officials until they are almost backed into a corner and forced to respond. During this time, they are gathering the knowledge in hopes to cast a striking blow when forced to respond. The knowledgeable passive parents often tend to be on the defensive so any correspondence that is eventually made is seldom of a positive nature. Such parents can be as dangerous as the omniscient parents, except that you do not encounter them as often. It still takes careful handling of situations with knowledgeable passive parents, because the wrong outcome can lead to damaging generalizations; much like the discussion about teachers existing for the purpose of picking on the students. It is important that knowledgeable passive parents, as well as the other types of parents discussed, are identified and steps are taken to move those parents away from the particular categorizations. Such could drastically improve the conditions in the learning environment so that other issues can be addressed.

Do not get the impression that the types of parents mentioned previously are the only types of parents. There are always exceptions to the rules. One category that the exceptional parents might fall under is the participant parent. This is the parent that gives you the most feedback. They are involved and concerned. These parents realize the important role they have in the education process and take the necessary steps to fulfill their duties. Yet, with this group, there are differences; which creates subcategories of unknowledgeable and knowledgeable participants. Unlike previous categories, participant parents do not have the day and night contrast.

The unknowledgeable participant parents may be the most innocent parents of all. They try hard to stay involved, only they lack the knowledge of procedure and protocol, and rely more on education officials; not to say that they give up their voice in the educational process. Unknowledgeable participants are interested in what officials think is the best course of action, but they also take care to monitor the progress and will inquire upon any inconsistencies that may occur. Though they are sometimes misinterpreted, unknowledgeable parents are not troublemakers. They are simply trying to learn the procedure so they can increase their involvement. In doing so, they may eventually move into the other category of participant parents, the knowledgeable participants.

The knowledgeable participant parents are the crown jewels of parents in the educational process.

Such parents continue to be a valued asset for years and place their personal stake in education. Knowledgeable participant parents are the parents you see on the committees and at the extra-curricular activities. By knowing the procedures, they act as an added support system to the education process as a whole. They also add to a more inviting learning environment. It is a desire that every parent falls under the category of being a knowledgeable participant parent. Such would bring about a positive momentum towards the ideal educational experience for all.

Now that general types of parents have been discussed, it is also important to address parent issues. Actually, saying parent issues leave the field wide-open; so one particular will be singled out. The simple question of who the parent believes—the teacher or the child—is a much debated topic. The issue itself is the main cause of rifts between home and school. It also is the issue that most often drives out the qualities that categorizes the type of parent the teacher is dealing with. For this reason, the problem is addressed at this time.

When dealing with the problem of whom the parent is to believe, let's first examine the two sides. Is it not the belief of the teacher that being the professional in the situation, there should not be any question as to whether he or she is telling to truth? Is it not the belief of the parent (in most cases) that if the child has been trustworthy, they will always be trustworthy? Can one say that it is wrong for the teacher to expect the parent to automatically side with him or her; or can one say that it is wrong for a parent to immediately take the side of the child, even if the parent plans to investigate the situation properly? Even though I am the educator, I have much sympathy for parents who are placed in such a situation under good measures. People give little credit to the students to be totally truthful at all times because it is difficult to know exactly what is going on with the child. However, is it also possible that the teacher has realized that what was said and done may not have been the most appropriate; but it is not too bad, so he or she can just change their wording slightly to get back across the appropriate line? I have seen each case happen, so I will not say that the teacher is hands down never wrong; neither will I say that a student should never be trusted. The only advice is to remain open to all possibilities until the truth is found (or at least the closest thing to it). I will attempt to explain my advice through an analogy. If water travels down a closed pipe, it will eventually all collect in one place. If water travels down an open pipe, the direction of the flow still depends on how the pipe is laying. No pipe means free-flowing water. The underlying meaning is that there are three directions that the conflict can go. Direction one is that you can be closed-minded and believe either side, and remain unchanged; neglecting to examine evidence (closed pipe). Direction two is that you take a side, but you are still willing to examine the evidence to find the truth (open pipe). Direction three is that you can take no side and simply go by the evidence presented to take a side (free-flowing). Clearly the first direction should not be the chosen route. The third direction would be the most objective; but take a look at the second direction. When the conflict arises, some parents already have an idea of who they believe, but they will still look at the evidence, just in case. The purpose is to find the truth, but does the second direction add unnecessary conflict? I describe it as the open pipe because the parent is open-minded; but does already having an idea of whom they believe sway their judgment a little? The second direction may not cause any conflict with clear evidence, but if the evidence is a little more complex, would there be a possibility that the parent eventually was led in the wrong direction unknowingly? Again, I have no side to take; I only

71

offer the argument to be carefully examined by all. One thought that I will offer on the matter is for parents to realize that a teacher might know their child a little more than expected. School is a different environment than home; which may prompt different and maybe even never seen before behaviors. Such can make a situation difficult because the parent is correct with saying that the child has never shown the behavior; but the parent must also remember that the condition under which the child is operating at school is drastically different from being at home. It is a very relevant argument in the interactions between the teacher and the parent; one that can control the climate on many levels. However, it comes with other factors that neither the parent nor teacher operates. Do we dare to explore?

Chapter 5: Administration – Blame Or Responsibility

It is easy to point the blame at a single person when searching for responsibility in any event of a break-down in the proper business of education. The question is, who's pointing the fingers? At whom are the fingers being pointed? All of the chaos involved in finding the responsible party has long since created an emotional web of defensive professionals. The truth is that no one wants to take the blame, but someone has to take the responsibility. The two must not be confused. When you take the blame, you are admitting to the weakness that led to the fall. When you take responsibility, you are showing the strength to get a handle on the failing situation and build it back to where it needs to be. I recall in the movie, *Spiderman,* there being a phrase, "with great powers lies great responsibility." The acceptance of a position of power calls for the acceptance of responsibility. Think about the state of education today; where does the responsibility exist? When scores do not meet the standards set in today's mandated legislation, who ends up being the one taken out of their position most often? When conflict among students arises, who makes the greater effort towards damage control? At this point, I will no longer speak around the topic; because the purpose is to go beyond boundaries and strike new ground in the discussion of education. It is clear that any negative outcome within the school settings is reflected back to the teacher. I am sure that principals, assistant principals, superintendents, and others get the toughest of verbal gnashing when there is a dip in the progression towards an ideal outcome; however, the brunt of action steps taken will most often fall on the teacher. I am sure that after a certain point, if a positive change has not come, the higher chain of command tends to see changes; but how is it compared to the changes that have taken place in the normal staff. I am fully aware that I should not talk about the administration. Is it not part of common decency for one whom is subordinate, to not speak out in protest? Though the topic may unfairly cast a shadow on the administration, it must be shaken up and awakened to reality. The reason this section has been addressed is because too often have teachers been re-assigned, suspended, or even fired for having an opinion. Fortunately, in milder cases, they may be encouraged to keep their opinions inside; facing no extreme act of reprimand. It leads the teacher to believe that they are not there to use their skill to further build upon structure of the educational process; rather, take the process and prove that they are capable of using it. Someone that might say that the statement is totally fabricated should look at how much one has actually had a say in a policy or procedural change that has taken place. Do not be fooled to think that because you had a lot to offer in the area of classroom ideas, your voice will be heard as clearly if you were at a board meeting that is discussing policy. The most power stays within the administration. The use of such power to support the teacher is needed more than one might think. It is true that teachers think with their hearts at times when they should use their heads; but remember that a teacher sees the job as caring for upwards of a hundred offspring. Teachers think like parents, and it should be respected more. I am not saying that anything a teacher says should become the new law, but every opinion should be considered.

The main point of the discussion is not to say that administration is not effective in its duties. It is also not say that the administration is actually the blame for the things that are placed on the teacher. It is more the method of dealing with the issues that is the problem. Many administrators (or maybe all) were classroom teachers at times, so I am certain that they can agree with the teacher's point of view. However, it happens that the administrator's method of damage control tends to be to extinguish the fire by covering it up. That is why the current section is titled "Why I shouldn't talk about the administration." Some may see this as damaging to some teachers and would try to cover it up in an act to protect the teacher. I think that stepping up and agreeing that teachers have the right to their opinion would be the better thing. The importance may not be seen unless the scope is widened. In all situations, it is better that all involved parties come to the table on the same level; everyone should be viewed as equally important. When there is no equality, power struggles ensues. More power creates an aggression and less power creates a submission. When a teacher is not supported on actions, he or she will undoubtedly fall into a submissive position (whether deliberate or not). The parent, in turn, gains an aggressive nature that will rear its face over and over until it is taken back to an equal state. The hardest part of the situation comes when the teacher is not backed by the administration; it interprets the stance as if the administration is actually siding with the parent. The previous situation only adds to the confusion and conflict. Should the administration believe that the teacher is right in any given situation? I think that the evidence in the matter should answer the question, but the administration should stand with the teacher until the issue is resolved; the reason being is that the employer should have faith that the person they hired is the most the competent person to carry out the duties and responsibilities involved. The administration has to stand by the confidence it possesses until proven otherwise. To some it is a small issue. Others may choose to stay out of certain situations as not to be falsely associated with the wrong thing. However, the truth stands alone. If the teacher is not truthful, the administrative stance still keeps the balance between the aggressive and submissive state and they still have the disclaimer of merely standing behind the teacher in good faith. If the teacher is truthful, everything works out anyway.

Going further, I dare to address legislation for the top of the hierarchy. It is the ultimate administrative position that has been key to fielding off education. Again, this chapter asks questions that may not normally get asked in a formal setting. The concern is the overarching power of federal legislation that has been handed down, such as the No Child Left Behind Act. Through the legislation, annual measurable objectives (AMO) are chosen to determine progress towards total achievement. Attendance is a major objective since being in class everyday maximizes instruction time. However, when there is a time of chronic misbehavior, a student is often placed in isolation within the school; not to ensure achievement, but to not count against the AMO. It upsets the balance of the learning environment and places the student in a condition with other offenders that could cause further incidence. Federal legislation is foundation that all educational processes are built around, but it is also putting up walls that ironically inhibit the growth demanded. It is not to sound anti-government; they are the higher power and are granted the justification for their insight. However, their responsibility is to listen to the voices that they represent and constantly work and revise legislation to maintain progress. It is just a matter of looking at the future implications of the matter at hand. Too often we jump into a plan of action without trying to look at things from different views.

Chapter 6: Welcome to Oz

To put all the ideas and people together to form a unified picture of what I have tried to express, let me introduce an analogy of Oz. It seems as if the education profession can be summed up in terms of themes from the movie, The Wizard of Oz. To me, this gives a major breakdown of what's wrong with the system and how to fix things.

There is no presence of home: What happens when it is difficult to contact parents, but procedure requires contact before and further disciplinary actions can be taken against the student? There is no working phone, which also may eliminate internet. Mailed letters are lost and never found. One cannot rely on the child to take letters home; basically a home visit is becoming a last resort (even though at times is inconvenient and sometimes unwise). In the classroom, discipline cannot be handled and the child continues to disrupt. In the age of blame the school for everything, administration fears lead to taking necessary actions as to cover themselves, but where does that leave the teacher and the students who deserve the privilege to have an uninterrupted learning experience? A very simple solution would be to involve child services immediately. If a child is developing a discipline record and the parent has not come to the school to straighten things out, I view that as a direct instance of neglect and should be handled accordingly. Yes, there will definitely be exceptions of single parents working three jobs that cannot get off in fear of losing the job, but going beyond the exceptions to care for your child may actually show that you care for the child and make a breakthrough in the behavior. Besides, a lot of negative behaviors come from the desire to get attention in the first place. If the child cannot come before everything else in a parent's life, why should the school continue to bend to cater to parents (strictly my opinion)?

No heart. The previous discussion could actually overlap into this analogy as well. There is not enough caring on the part of many. There is not enough compassion that is needed in a profession that is so involved with children. Today's society is so self-centered that in some instances, not even religion can remedy the need for unconditional caring for all. We tend to think with our pockets; not even with our heads and definitely not with our hearts. Certainly the children should be our top priority, but legislation has a narrow view that benefits the students, and not the situation. One must realize that in a situation, if not all parties are served, an issue cannot be resolved. My example comes from a recent proposal on education to grant merit raises for teachers. Merit raises are child-centered in the fact that it forces accountability to the teacher (who, of course, needs to be pressured into making a student learn as if his or her present credentials cannot be trusted). To some, the move is perfect and guaranteed. However, how does it look to a teacher who cares so much about children that he goes into inner city or rural schools where achievement seems to be an uphill battle? His efforts to change lives seem to be boundless, but legislation says it is not enough. A matter like this may force a small change within the system but it binds the radical change agents, which are teachers who step far outside the box to make a monumental difference. It makes a teacher who really goes beyond to care for students, wonder why he should care instead of just falling in line and paying his bills; a sad end to what could have been an extraordinary experience for his students.

No Brain. This analogy is not meant to be insulting; it just infers a lack of complete analysis of solutions for the problems we face in education. This topic can coincide with the previous topic, but let's explore even more. It seems that whenever subject of school improvement appears, the x-factor is the teacher; change the teacher, change the schools. We need more accountability for teachers; merit raises for teachers; parent choice of schools with the best teachers. This is the thinking of most people today. It sounds logical enough…if the teachers were the only people involved in education. If schools stood as independent entities where teachers were at the top of the hierarchy and there were no administrators, superintendents, secretaries of education, or even parents, we would be on to something. It seems farfetched, but think about all the things that influence achievement; it is not only having expert instructors and challenging curriculum. A child's home life influences beliefs, attitudes, personality, and motivation. Having no home life, would definitely change circumstances. However, that is impossible, so we have to logically balance such influences with the teacher's accountability. Parent and student choice that is demanded so much needs to be balanced with parent and student accountability. Let's take merit pay for teachers as an example. Merit pay would improve teacher accountability, why not have merit tax breaks for parents whose students achieve highly or even students who have a low rate of disciplinary actions taken against them; and of course for students, have grants and scholarships based on academic achievement (guaranteed, not so competitive much like today's scholarships). Furthermore, there should be parent and student accountability for lack of effort as well; mandatory counseling or parenting classes for parents with students that have frequent documentation of disciplinary issues. There may also be disciplinary action given to the parent as frequently as it has been handed to the student. Placing a parent with a severely delinquent child in a very inconvenient position would cause them to go great lengths to get out of the situation. I know that there are some students that even their parents cannot control them and these are prime candidates for quick, extensive and meaningful intervention. In all, it should not seem illogical, but should operate through common sense and a sense of reality.

Cowardly. There is a difference between catering to the needs of students and exceptionalities and enabling negative behaviors. The line between what is expected of school systems to provide students and what parents and family members pressure the systems into doing is narrow. The single most terrifying kryptonite of the school systems are lawsuits. The school system is a human operated institution that is held to super-human expectations, to satisfy every single person. When one person feels less "spoiled" than the next, there is always a threat to take the matter to the courts. Let's say that we have a scenario where a student has been kicked out of school because of chronic misbehavior. There is an established policy that all possible alternatives must be attempted and the parent realizes that the policy is so open that he or she makes up any step that could have been an alternative to help win the case—animal therapy might work for the student. Okay, the alternative stated may push the envelope a little, but the point is that openness in policies takes the power from the system into the unpredictable hands of parents. Schools systems must develop the most concrete policies possible to stand against few parents who just want to pick a fight. The problem happens when the parent wins and causes more and more parents to pick fights until it seems the parents control the schools and issues are almost impossible to resolve. What parents don't know is that they are presenting more dangers to their children by not allowing the school to create firm policies that can stand against the extreme cases, leaving them to wreak havoc constantly.

The Wizard. Here we have a magical being in power to solve all of the mysteries that lie within the field of education. I see this as the federal legislation that comes from politicians, not educators who are in the classroom everyday and have a first-person view of what is really going on. As we see from the renowned tale, the wizard consists of mainly smoke and mirrors; a man behind a curtain. However, continue to follow me if you think that what I am stating is a bad thing. Through further analysis, you see that the intentions of the man behind the curtain are for the better; his persona just has been lost in midst of astronomical expectations. Just as in the movie, it is time to expose the wizard at face value so that the practical solutions are realized. That way we all discover the answers that may be right in front of our eyes, which have been blinded previously by the mysticism of politics and special interest.

The Witch. This analogy will be addressed in brevity. The question is, who plays the witch in education? Who exists as the wicked entity out for power and influence over the weak and innocent? I have all faith that no group as a whole acts against the achievement of students and the success of education. However, those whose lives are built around the harassment of school officials, faculty and staff would be wicked. I have come across parents who look to find the next person that they can chew out in order to build their own egos. I have seen teachers with underlying hate and prejudice, but have bills that influence their false acts of sincerity. I have seen power hungry administrators whose descriptions match the definition previously stated in the opening of the section. The introduction of wickedness has steered education down the yellow brick road of school improvement. The hope is to find logic, compassion, courage, and a sense of home in education.

Chapter 7: If Education Was a Pill

Is this book to call out the higher powers or to put people in their place? It is certainly not. The purpose of the book is for people to start talking; to encourage people to open their eyes to other viewpoints and make educated decisions. If you have been paying attention, you will notice that the book does not support any one viewpoint. I wrote from a personal perspective, but I offered the explanations for different views. This book is to dig into the world of a teacher, but it also attempts to connect it to the world of others involved in the learning process.

If you are still with me at this point of the book, I hope that the questions and concerns spewing from your minds, will cause some engaging conversation. Actually, if you are anything like me, you would think that there has been plenty of argument of the problem, but wonder where are the enduring solutions that make the argument justifiable? Unfortunately, I cannot present a chapter for solutions that were well referenced or experimented like the creed, but I will offer my thoughts based on observations and life experiences. What can we do for our children? First of all, I do remind the reader that this is not to lay blame or to name names. I want to be a facilitator of the conversation for positive change. However, the only way for change to come, one must be acceptant of change. My first suggestion is for all involved parties - parents, teachers, administrators, communities, politicians, and even students - to include a belief of change as being good in their belief systems. The greatest barrier in conflict of various natures has been resistance to change. However, some of the greatest events and memorable turning points in history came about through the desire or acceptance of change. The world evolves constantly and so should the system that prepares the young to face the changing world. It is not wrong to accept the fact that we have to do things differently than we did fifty, ten, or even five years ago. One thing that must be changed is the traditional role of the teacher. I can honestly say that when I was a student, I've always had the same idea about a teacher. It was almost as if they were not human. I also get the same reaction from the students that I teach. It seems that they are surprised to see teachers in "regular" clothes or even in public. It is almost as if teachers do not exist outside of being inside the classroom. It is such a misconception that it actually causes a disconnection between the teacher and the student. I think that one job that a teacher has is to take it upon him or herself to bridge that gap. It goes beyond trying a new teaching strategy; it is also being conscious and sensitive to the social culture of the students. One thing that I have learned is that by stepping outside of that traditional role, I get more respect from my students because they see me as being more relatable. Also, being aware of the social culture helps the approach with issues that a child might have with another student. To a teacher who is not educated on the social culture of a student, it may almost sound like students are talking in another language. There may be a conflict or some form of inappropriate actions happening in front of the teacher that he or she may not know if the language that is being used, cannot be understood. So knowledge of social culture has its advantages on many levels.

How can the administration take a bigger part in creating a solution? To me it is simple. First, the hiring process needs to be created around criteria that leaves the ultimate confidence that the teacher hired for a position will do the job that is desired. Such would hopefully build a confidence in the teachers that the administrators could stand by in any situation. A greater confidence is needed to put the teachers' anxieties at ease when coming against the obstacles in which they face on a daily basis. In any profession, it is apparent that a confident worker is an efficient worker. Just like the misconception between students and teachers, there is also a misconception between teachers and administration. No matter how friendly an administrator may seem, there is always a tension in their presence caused by the thought that they are monitoring your every move to catch you doing something wrong. The explanation that I offer for the previously stated issue can be described as the frustration pyramid. At the top are the officials whose job it is to come up with the "solutions", as asked for by the ones who support them. Their decisions are passed down the pyramid to make certain that they are implemented. The next level then passes the decisions down below them; stressing the importance of accomplishing the objective that was passed. Unfortunately, the teacher lands at the bottom of the pyramid and receives the compounded pressure of achieving the desired goal. At the bottom, the responsibility and the accountability has piled so much that it causes elevated levels of frustration for the teacher, which can affect the relationship between the teacher and the administration.

There are teachers who lack the confidence that the administration is there for support and see their job as being to pick out the teacher's flaws and expose them in order to mold the perfect teacher. The lack of confidence in the superior is what has brought about a disconnection between the administration and the teachers. If it takes a more strenuous interviewing process to find a candidate that is "hands down" the best for the position then so be it. However I am quite sure that the certification process filters through those who do not quite measure up. It should be no question that the person in the position is doing all that is within his or her power to make the best experience for all students with no intent toward incidence. Though it may seem that I am speaking against administration, I do want to emphasize that it is the teacher's job to do whatever it takes to provide the best experience with no intent toward incidence! They should never put themselves in a position that might lead to them being questioned on professionalism. I know that we do not live in a perfect world where nothing would go wrong, but we should not invite occurrences. This would potentially lead administration not to take a damage control perspective of their job and allow them room to stand behind the confidence of their employment. It is not a one sided street in any means and I certainly hope that no one gathered the impression of such as they read through the book. I do speak as a teacher, but I also express the point that we cannot be held blameless in any way.

As I continue, I definitely do not wish to leave anyone out of the conversation. I guess the next discussion would be explaining my thoughts on the parents' role in the solution to our problem. The particular subject is difficult to address because we have so many differences in the make-up of our family structure. It is understood that speaking of parents, I also include guardians, who may not even be related to the child, but is responsible for the child's welfare. So what is their role? It certainly seems as if the parents have more power in the world of education. Certainly changes come about when parents voice concerns. The students, in most cases, yield to parent/guardian request more than some teachers' requests (especially with the existence of the student-teacher disconnect theory). It is no doubt that the parents and the guardians make a huge difference in the state of education. Perhaps the biggest contribution is the fact that students bring values, beliefs, and routines from their home life directly into the schools. It can even be concluded that much of (if not all) of the behavior that happens in school correlates directly with behavior at home. The respect or disrespect; the organization or disorganization; the good hygiene or bad hygiene; all can be directly related to what goes on at home. You may ask, what about the kids that are taught the right thing and do the right thing at home; but when they get to school, they feel more freedom to stray away from their values, causing them to act out? The resulting actions can still be seen as a gap in structure at home. Sometimes parents can push the line too far that a child may actually behave out of fear more than respect; but once given a little room, will try to run all over the unsuspecting teacher. Parents must be fully aware of the impact of home life and work at presenting the best example at home to be taken to school. Of course we know that there are cases of abuse, neglect, and other terrifying events that a child has to go through. Those moments are when the school actually will have to step in for the parents. I do not just mean counselors or mentors that meet with them periodically to talk; such does not seem natural. I am talking about feeding them when they are not being properly nourished; supplying clothes to them when their parents want to spend their money on crack. Shocked? Don't be. I know the first thing is that there is not enough money to do anything like that realistically. Do you think those teachers who are actually taking money from their pockets to do just that, would agree? If we want to take full responsibility for the education of our children, we have to make some real changes.

The question of the hour to me is, "Can we get to the point where no child is left behind?" I add this question in the solution section because it is given the credit for being the remedy to the ills of education. I have long thought through this question, but I cannot shake the belief that regardless of all the standards, objectives, or interventions (short of divine intervention), there will always be some students who fall through the cracks. Should we do everything that we can to try to prevent the grim outcome? Yes. Should we be held accountable for the outcome, no matter how hard we try, in order to save face for unrealistic ideas put through in hasty legislation? No. I will not say that I do not have the same desire for every student that I teach to go on, be prosperous and live happy, meaningful lives. But to single-handedly mandate that every single child in a nation's education system will be given the desire, motivation, and resources to meet or exceed standards to me is reaching levels of super-human capabilities that no mortal man possesses. Education is not as simple as inserting a chip into a child's brain with the knowledge; it involves a combination of intrinsic and extrinsic institutions. We can always put on the greatest show around with dogs, ponies, and flashing lights; but if a child has it instilled in his mind that school is not for him, they can set up internal barriers that will block any efforts to help or "save" them. What would be the remedy for that? I don't think that any child should be left behind, but I do think that some children want to be left behind. Sadly, the backgrounds from which some children come have been those that groom them to become the statistic. They are helpless to fight against it because for some, it is simply their way of life. Where is the legislation that will curtail a destructive environment before it has its effect on the child? Find the solution and I would agree that no child will be left behind.

By now you probably think that there is no way that I could be a teacher, the way that I seemingly pick the profession apart. I will proclaim that my passion for teaching drives the discussion. If I did not care, I would not address the issues. My heart goes out to the children more than anything else. They are the biggest stakeholders in the education system. I think that they also have a very important (if not the biggest) role in the solution of education. Education would be flawless if every child that entered a school building came in with an eagerness to learn that would cause them to beg for opportunities to expand their knowledge. Oddly enough I do not think that it is impossible to stir the kind of motivation in students that would drive them to seek out knowledge and not wait for it to be fed to them. I can remember that amidst the chaos of growing up in public housing with seven brothers and sisters, I maintained a drive to remain educated. I will not say that I was perfect. I did seek temporary solutions that are typically of people who have immediate needs that are hard to get met. I engaged in some of the stereotypical acts that are associated with people who come from the projects. With the uncertainty of how I would get the things I needed, I could have fallen into the path of trying to find the easy way out (no matter how illegal); however, the desire to get an education became my chosen path and has been the drive of my life ever since. I never considered myself the exception because I did not have some miraculous event that became the turning point of my life. I just remember developing a dream to be better and using my education to make the dream a reality. This is a strong example of the power of education. We have to look beyond the perfect curriculum and the most competitive standards. We need to assess the dreams of the students and base our instruction around empowering the students to work towards their dreams, no matter what it may be. So my ultimate solution is this: teach purpose through the fulfillment of dreams and they will eventually understand that a broad body of knowledge can only enhance the dream; then they would appreciate the value of a total education rather than just wanting what they think would be relevant to a particular career. It seems as if we want to build a model student from the outside-in (presenting a perfectly structured curriculum that will push a student toward his or her dream) rather than motivate a student to build a life from the inside-out (using dreams to drive the desire to want an education). If we are going to take the outside-in approach, we must also clarify the role of the education system. Right now it confuses teachers as to whether it is a business or an institution. Deciding between the two may actually help with the problem of education. If it exists as a business, the education system could relieve its employees of the pain it takes to intertwine curriculum through the beliefs, values, backgrounds, etc; and just provide a mass curriculum that would generate an efficient product in the form of the perfect scholar and the rest would go to waste. There would be no need for differentiation between multiple intelligences, Bloome's taxonomy, multicultural education, nor anything that caters to the differences and individualism that is unique to every single student that enters a school. Therefore, if the education system is going to continually function as a business, we should rid our teachers of the extra time and effort it takes to present such a diverse curriculum.

If the education system is to be an institution of learning, the teacher should be respected as a capable facilitator of knowledge and is free of the scrutiny of politically driven and unrealistic standards. If the institution is supposed to stand as the embodiment of education, shouldn't there also exist a local and internal control of purpose? Such would mean that the confidence in the teacher hired to do a job is all that stands as the structure by which they operate. If teachers are to accommodate multiple intelligences and learning styles, they should not be strapped to the rails of strict standards and timelines that are used to prove their worth rather than looking at genuine outcomes of the students to show the teacher's worth. If education was a pill that the students could take and automatically acquire the knowledge, the problem would be solved. However, students are rarely on the same exact schedule with regard to mastery of particular concepts, and teachers must re-structure instruction and pace to try to encompass every student; but the shape of the open arms that teachers stretch, don't fit in the narrow windows that administrators create as a result of legislation passed down. The present blend of purpose in the education system is certainly a major source of the chaos that is so heavily debated. I undoubtedly believe that a clear distinction between business and institution would make a teacher's job easier if not just simplifying the educational process. It definitely would decrease the uncertainty that surrounds education; leading to the conversations that picks the entire institution apart; where there are so many opinions and criticisms. But the message is simple; it takes more than one person to ensure a prosperous educational experience for a child. We should not take each other's role for granted.

So, what is wrong with education? Who is to blame for what is wrong? I set out to show that the only real problem we have in education is that not enough students want it as much as they should. Everything else stems from the previous statement. Since students don't want an education, it becomes a question of who takes the responsibility to change the pessimistic mentality. This is where the teachers are put out on a limb with a type of support that sometimes questions the worth of being in the education field. Sure the experts have done the research over and over to develop the standards that is then backed by powerful legislation. The lawmakers force the teachers to live by the standards. And if the proper results are not accomplished, it is times up for the teacher. Despite the growing responsibilities and expectations, teachers remain dedicated to trying to secure a future for every single child with which he or she comes into contact with. Why not spread the responsibility? As an extreme scenario, why not even share the responsibility with gamers and media? We can encourage them to support education in ways that students would not detect as education. If children are going to continue to play the gangster and violent video games where the character sells drugs, make it necessary for them to calculate their revenue. It may be a drastic example, but if you seriously think about whether or not the child would continue to play the game under the given circumstances, the example might seem more logical than it sounded.

In a sense, the education field is filled with constant change. Many teachers have commented that everyday something new can be expected. Despite the constant change, teachers have a monumental task of adapting to a streamlined set of standards prescribed by federal, state, and local officials. It takes much effort and talent to be a teacher and adapt to change, at the same time, sticking to the persistent and pervasive guidelines that frame the educational process. However, teachers unyieldingly commit to doing the job asked of them. As a teacher, I go further to say that all that is asked for in return is an equal amount of appreciation with the amount of criticism and accountability demanded. Evidence of years of experience should show that there is no question of how far a teacher will go to make sure that a child has the greatest learning experience. The proof should tell others that it is okay to trust a teacher's judgment without building more and more pressure until they are beaten into submission. If the trend continues, it is sad to see the outcome. For now, it still remains that teaching is more than a profession; it is indeed a calling, much like how some say they are called to be ministers. It is not a business as much as it is a necessity to everyone's way of life. As it continues to be scrutinized, it will also continue to be marginalized and marketed. The end result just might be the perfect teacher that society demands teachers to be today. However, the education profession will also be filled teachers with no souls; no real care or concern for the students. The teacher will be too involved with presenting the perfect routine with the perfect visuals and the perfect script to produce the perfect student. Unfortunately, with the overflow of emotions that children contain as they enter the classroom, they will be more disconnected than ever before. Still, with the increase of standards for curriculum, the mandating of standardized tests, the involuntarily enforcement of legislation, and the increased requirements for certification, one can clearly see how the education field is transforming into an unrecognizable entity. And with so many instances where other professions are compared to teaching, there is one question to pose. How many other professions have undergone a complete and unwarranted metamorphosis that was not of any capitalistic purpose? Sure all people in a competitive society want to adapt to the changing times, but isn't education supposed to be a cooperative institution? Let's not think that there is no capitalistic motivation involved in the education field. The only problem is that it exists for the wrong reasons and it just might be the answer to what is wrong with education. We must realize that education is too important to turn into the newest marketing strategy to gain wealth; but if it ever becomes a victim of a complete and total meltdown, what will be the far-reaching consequences?

We are all in this together and the children most important. I do believe that all students are capable of learning and it is our job to instill in them a desire to learn. As teachers, we must think mainly of the students. As parents, we must be open participants and continue the process at home. As administrators, we must trust and support our judgment of those whom we hire and maintain local control of our educational process. As a community, we must support our children, parents, teachers, and schools, continuing to present an equal atmosphere for all. As a society, we must open our eyes to the ways of the world and take back our existence through the power of education. We must uncover the truths and beliefs that can help us reach our life's goal and make it part of our over-arching philosophy, so that they no longer have to be underground.

KB

KOBALT BOOKS

www.**kobaltbooks**.com

www.ingramcontent.com/pod-product-compliance
Lightning Source LLC
Chambersburg PA
CBHW071132090426
42736CB00012B/2096